The Promised Hope... starts with a baby's first cry

A Christmas Musical for Every Choir

Creator and Arranger
TOM FETTKE

Orchestrator
RUSSELL MAULDIN

Performance Time: 38 minutes

lillenas
PUBLISHING COMPANY

lillenas.com

Contents

The Promised Hope – Opening

Choir

Words and Music by
STEVEN CURTIS CHAPMAN,
TOM FETTKE and RUSSELL MAULDIN
Arranged by Tom Fettke

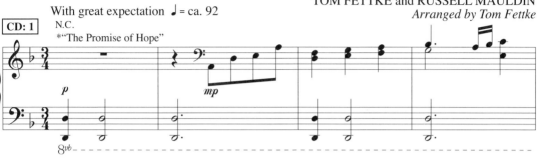

*Music by TOM FETTKE and RUSSELL MAULDIN. Copyright © 2010 by Pilot Point Music (ASCAP).
All rights reserved. Administered by The Copyright Company, PO Box 128139, Nashville, TN 37212-8139.

Do Not
Photocopy

*"Night Before Christmas"

Christ Is Come

Choir

Words and Music by
LOWELL ALEXANDER
and **MARK HAUTH**
Arranged by Tom Fettke

*"Joy to the World"

CD: 4

Lord and King o-ver us a-bid - ing. Mer - ci - ful and

just is He; Christ will reign_ in_ vic - to - ry,

Christ will reign in_ vic - to - ry!

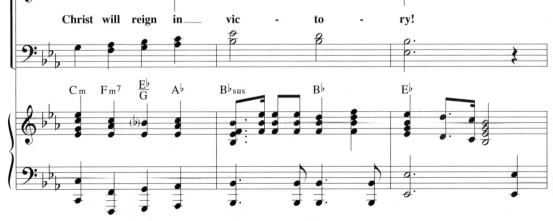

Night Before Christmas

Solo and Choir

Words and Music by
STEVEN CURTIS CHAPMAN
Arranged by Tom Fettke

NARRATOR: Though you are small, Bethlehem . . . , out of you will come One who will be ruler over Israel. He will stand and shepherd His flock in the strength of the Lord, in the majesty of the Lord His God. And they will live securely, for then His greatness will reach to the ends of the earth. And He will be their peace . . . O Bethlehem, the hopes and fears of all the years are met in you tonight. *Micah 5 NIV para and "O Little Town of Bethlehem" by Phillips Brooks*

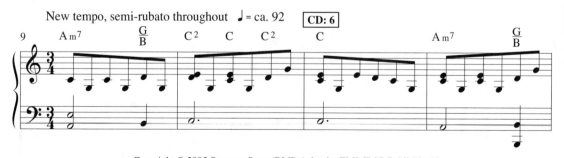

MEDIUM VOICE SOLO

73

wait - ed, the hope of the a - ges would

wait - ed, the hope of the a - ges would

77

break with the dawn. And the song that all of cre -

break with the dawn. And the song that all of cre -

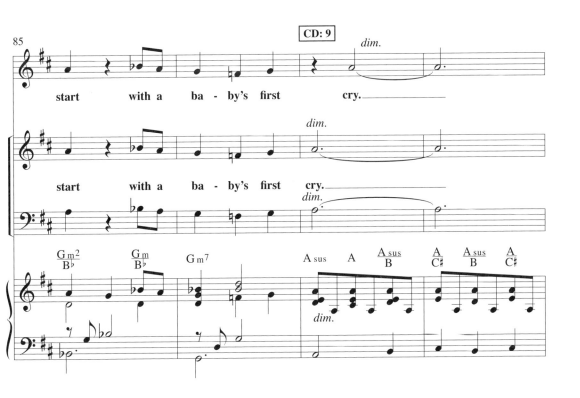

81
a - tion was an - tic - i - pat - ing would
a - tion was an - tic - i - pat - ing would
A4 2 A A/G D/F♯ C/G G
85
CD: 9
dim.
start with a ba - by's first cry.
start with a ba - by's first cry.
dim.
dim.
Gm2/B♭ Gm/B♭ Gm7 A sus A A sus/B A/C♯ A sus/B A/C♯
dim.

And on the night be - fore Christ - mas___

Ma - ry laid down to rest,

Oo,___ Oo,___

While Jo - seph, he paced the floor pray-ing.__

Oo,_____

D | D/C# | Bm Bm2 Bm7 | F#m/A | G

And in an ev - 'ry - day sta - ble___

Oo,_____

G 2(no3) | Bm7 | A2/C# | D | D2

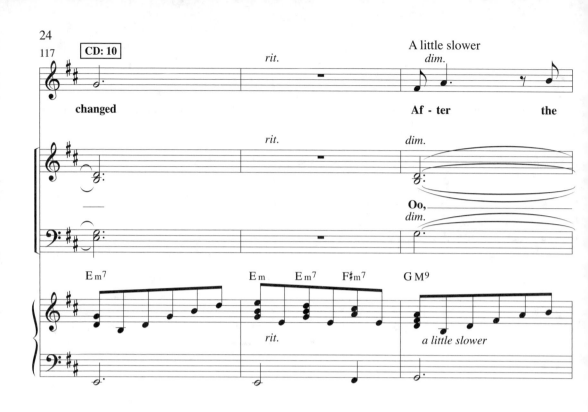

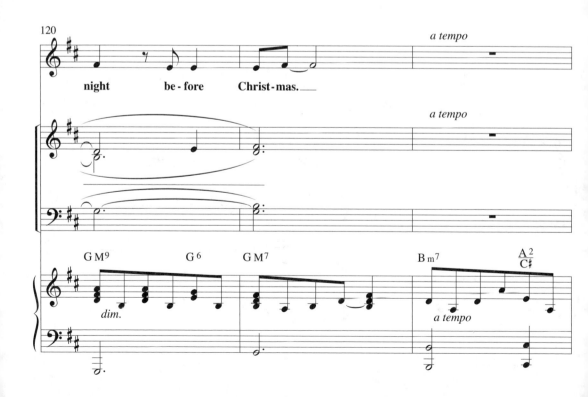

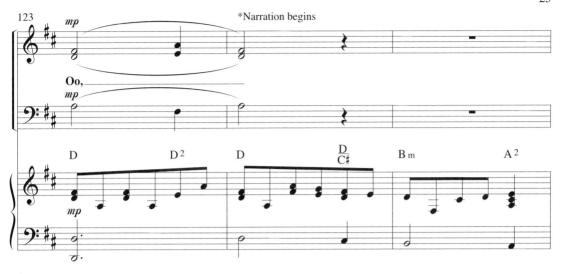

*NARRATOR: While Mary and Joseph were in Bethlehem,
the time came for the baby to be born, and she gave birth to
her firstborn, a Son . . . and His name was Jesus. *Luke 2:6-7* NIV *para*

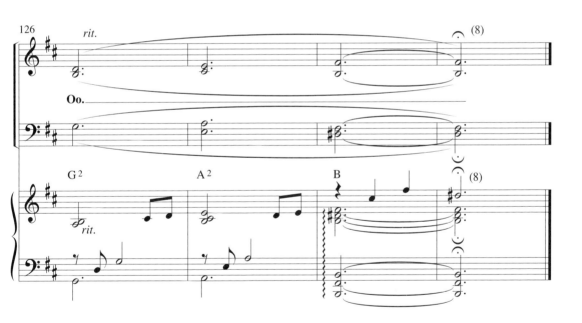

Angels, from the Realms of Glory

Choir

JAMES MONTGOMERY

STEVEN CURTIS CHAPMAN
Arranged by Tom Fettke

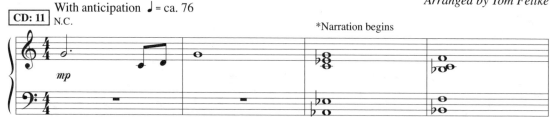

NARRATOR: An angel said to the shepherds, "Do not be afraid. I bring you good tidings of great joy that will be for all the people. Today in the city of David a Savior has been born to you; He is Christ the Lord. This will be a sign to you: You will find a baby wrapped in swaddling clothes and lying in a manger." Suddenly a great company of the heavenly host appeared with the angel, praising God and saying, "Glory to God in the highest, and on earth peace, goodwill towards men."

Luke 2:8-14 NIV para

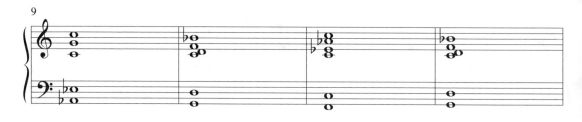

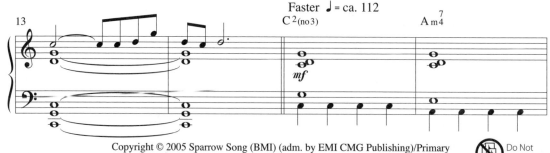

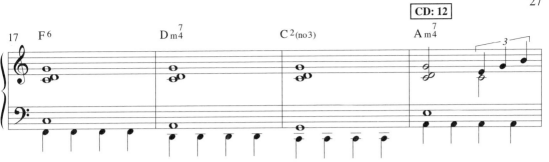

CD: 16

72

Christ, the new - born King.

Tho' an in - fant

now we view Him, He shall fill His Fa - ther's throne.

Gath-er all the na-tions to Him; Ev-'ry knee__ shall

then bow down.__

All cre-a - tion joins in prais-ing God the Fa - ther,

Spir - it, Son._____ Ev-er-more your voic-es rais - ing

to the e - ter - nal Three in One.

Come and wor - ship,_____ Come and

Jesus, O What a Wonderful Child

Choir

Words and Music
African American Spiritual
**Arranged by Tom Fettke*

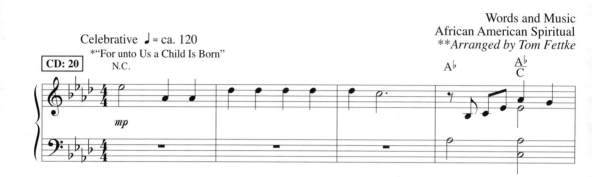

*NARRATOR: "To us a child is born, to us a son is given,
and the government will be on his shoulders. And he
will be called Wonderful Counselor, Mighty God,
Everlasting Father, Prince of Peace." *Isaiah 9:6 NIV*

*Words from Isaiah 9:6; Music by GEORGE FREDERICK HANDEL.
**Thanks to Thomas Grassi for his contributions to the creation of this arrangement.

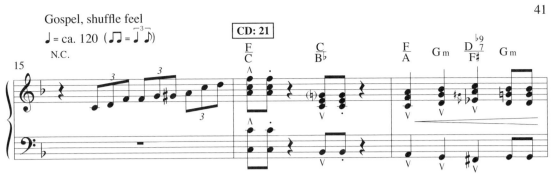

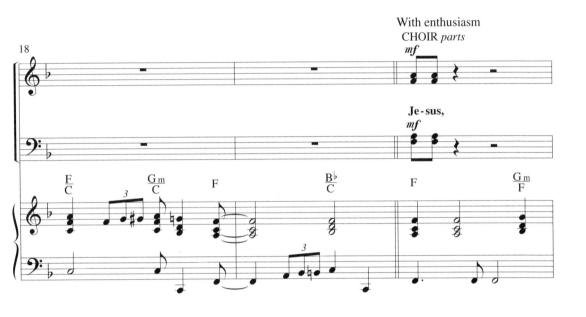

Child. Je-sus, Je-sus, so

low-ly,___ meek and mild.___ New life, new hope, new

joy___ He brings;___ Won't you lis-ten to the

lis-ten   to the   an-gels   sing.___   Glo-ry,   glo-ry,

glo   -   ry   to the   new   -   born___   King.___

For   un-to   us   a   Child   is

Born Where the Shadows Lie

Solo and Choir

Words and Music by
KEITH and KRISTYN GETTY
Arranged by Tom Fettke

NARRATOR: In the beginning was the Word, and the Word was with God, and the Word was God. The Word became flesh and lived for a while among us. We have see His glory, the glory of the One and Only Son, who came from the Father, full of grace and truth. John 1:1, 14 NIV para

PLEASE NOTE: Copying of this product is NOT covered by CCLI licenses. For CCLI information call 1-800-234-2446.

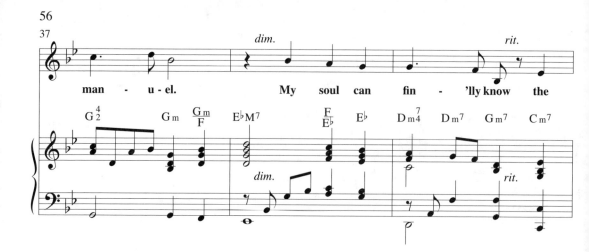

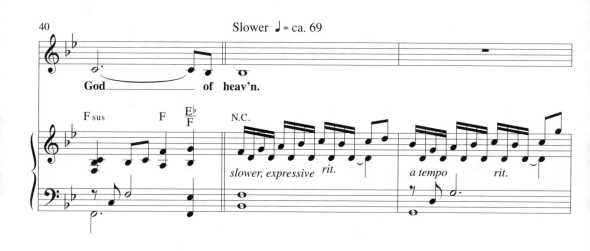

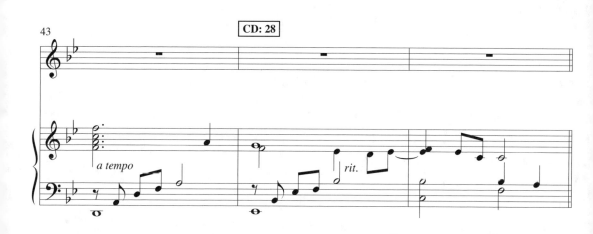

Faster ♩ = ca. 84

mf

Born with a road a-head; a - lone those

mp Oo, Oo,

mp

B♭2 C2/B♭ C/B♭ F/A

faster

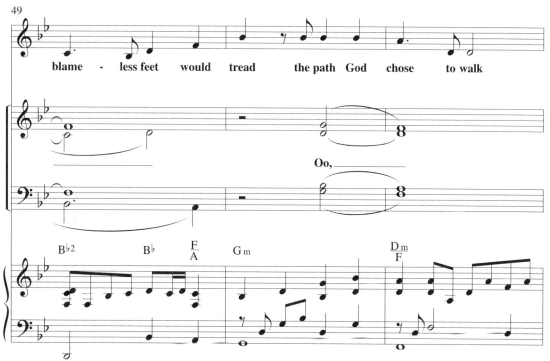

blame - less feet would tread the path God chose to walk

Oo,

B♭2 B♭ F/A Gm Dm/F

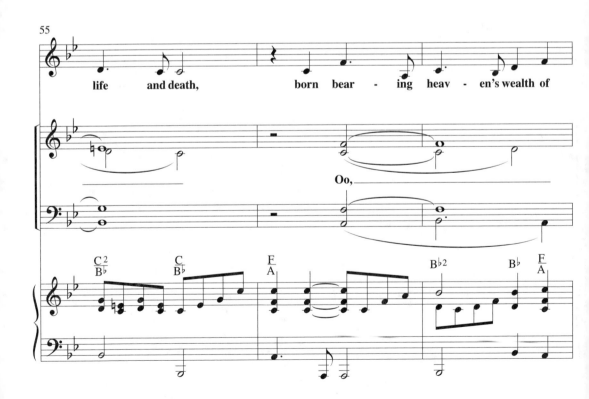

CD: 29

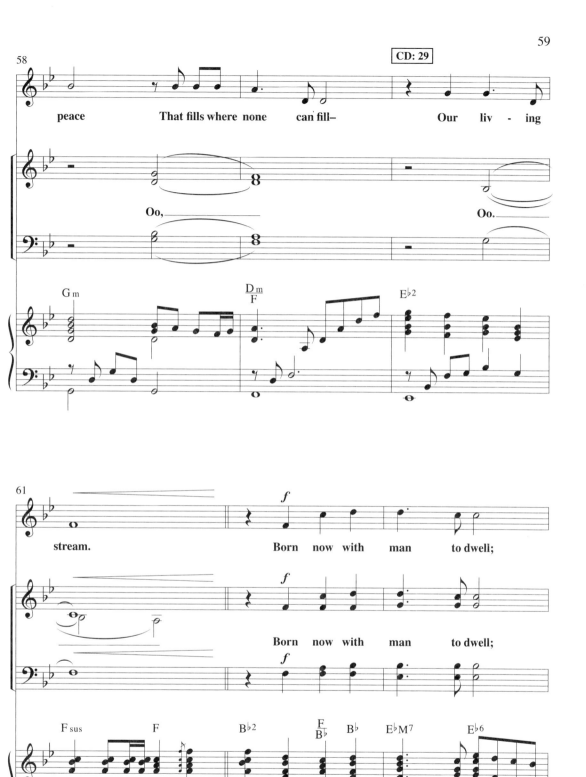

peace   That fills where none   can fill—   Our   liv - ing

Oo,_____   Oo._____

Gm   Dm/F   E♭2

stream.   Born   now   with   man   to dwell;

Born   now   with   man   to dwell;

F sus   F   B♭2   F/B♭   B♭   E♭M7   E♭6

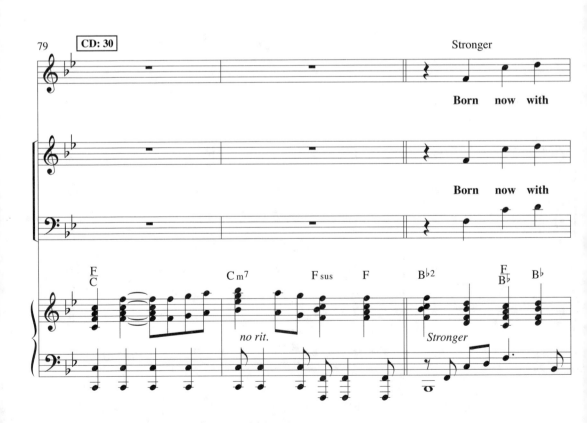

88

us.   Born now with man   to dwell;

us.   Born now with man   to dwell;

F sus   F   B♭2   F/B♭   B♭   E♭M7   E♭6

91

rit.   ten.   *a tempo*   *dim. poco a poco*

Our Lord Im - man - u - el.   My soul can

rit.   ten.   *a tempo*   *dim. poco a poco*

Our Lord Im - man - u - el.   My soul can

ten.   *dim. poco a poco*

F   D♭9/7   D7   G4/2   Gm   Gm/F   E♭M7   F/E♭   E♭

rit.   ten.   *a tempo*   *dim. poco a poco*

Soon and Very Soon

Choir

Words and Music by
ANDRAE CROUCH
**Arranged by Tom Fettke*

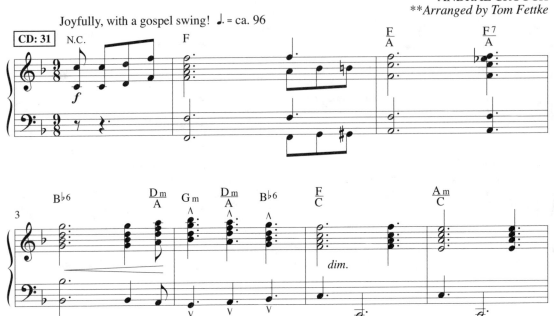

*NARRATOR: After Jesus was born in Bethlehem of Judea, during
the time of King Herod, Magi from the east came to Jerusalem and
asked, "Where is the one who has been born king of the Jews? We
saw his star in the east and have come to worship him." After
they were told the Christ was to be born in Bethlehem of Judea,
they went on their way. And the star they had seen in the east went
ahead of them until it stopped over the place where the child was.
When they saw the star, they were overjoyed. *Matt. 2:1-2, 9-10 NIV para*

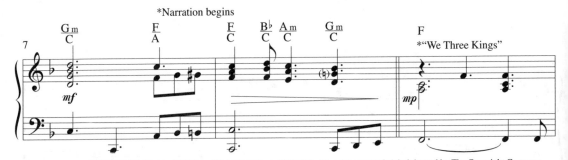

*Music by JOHN H. HOPKINS, JR. Arr. © 2010 by Pilot Point Music (ASCAP). All rights reserved. Administered by The Copyright Company,
PO Box 128139, Nashville, TN 37212-8139.
**Thanks to Thomas Grassi for his contributions to the creation of this arrangement.

CD: 32

Soon and ver - y soon

we are going to see the King.___

CD: 36

Sovereign Lord

Choir

Words and Music by
TOM FETTKE
Arranged by Tom Fettke

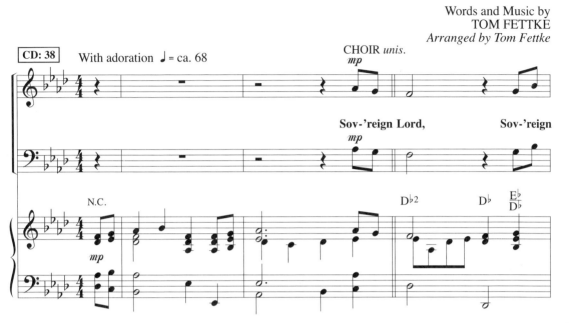

Do Not
Photocopy

*Narration begins

Lord.

*NARRATOR: On coming to the house, the Magi saw the child
with His mother Mary, and they bowed down and worshipped
Him. Then they opened their treasures and presented Him
with gifts of gold and of incense and myrrh. *Matt. 2:11* NIV *para*

CD: 39

Sov - 'reign   Lord,   Sov - 'reign

mp

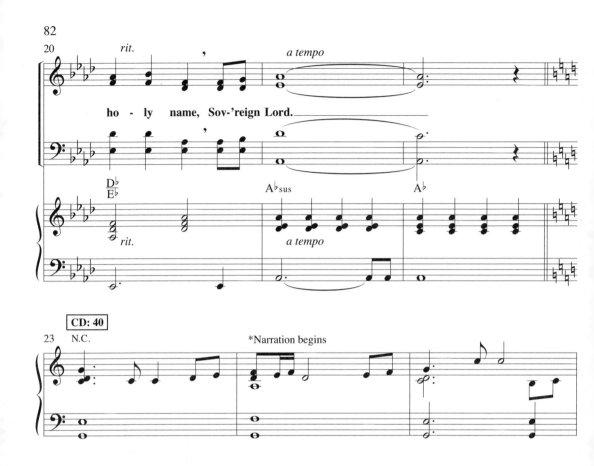

ho - ly name, Sov-'reign Lord.

CD: 40

*Narration begins

*NARRATOR: Great Creator, God and Savior, King of kings
and Lord of lords– All creation stands to worship You and
fills the sky with endless Alleluias. We, Your people, bow
before You lifting honor, praise and blessing . . . Lord, the
goal of all we aspire to, now and forever, is You; and the
reality of Your glory and grace. *-From "Jesus" by Ken Bible, altered*
© 1998 Pilot Point Music (ASCAP)

Faster ♩ = ca. 108

Segue to "Gloria"

Gloria

(Christmas version)
Praise Team or Trio and Optional Choir

Words and Music by
JONAS MYRIN, MATT REDMAN
and PETER KVINT
Arranged by Tom Fettke

High praise ♩ = ca. 108

CD: 41

N.C.

mp

Narration ends   C   G

Em⁷   Dsus

PRAISE TEAM *or* TRIO *(Optional Choir)*
mp

The skies are filled with Your glo - ry,

mp

G²

CD: 44

glo - ry and grace, O God.

CHOIR *may join*

Glo - ri - a! Glo - ri -

a! Heav - en and earth sing how

PRAISE TEAM *or* TRIO

Come and Worship – A Celebration

Choir and Optional Congregation

Arranged by Tom Fettke

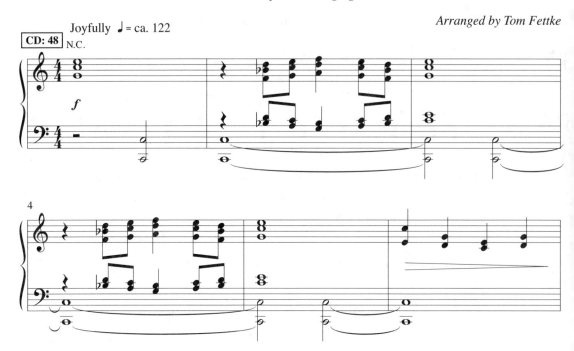

NARRATOR: Shout for joy to the LORD, all the earth, burst into jubilant song with vibrant music . . . Celebrate! For I bring you good news of great joy . . . Today in the city of David a Savior has been born to you. He is Christ the Lord. Rejoice!

Ps. 98:4 and Luke 2:10-11 NIV para

*"Hark! the Herald Angels Sing"
CONGREGATION *may join*

Christ,   the new-born   King.   Come   and

wor - ship   Christ,   the new-born   King.